OPENING *Intuition*
BOOK 5

INTRODUCTION TO
PSYCHIC ART AND
PSYCHIC READINGS

AN EASY-TO-USE, STEP-BY-STEP ILLUSTRATED GUIDEBOOK

LUCY BYATT   KIM ROBERTS

FINDHORN PRESS

LUCY BYATT & KIM ROBERTS 2017
THE RIGHT OF LUCY BYATT AND KIM ROBERTS TO BE IDENTIFIED AS THE AUTHORS OF
THIS WORK HAS BEEN ASSERTED BY THEM IN ACCORDANCE WITH THE COPYRIGHT,
DESIGNS AND PATENTS ACT 1998.

PUBLISHED IN 2017 BY FINDHORN PRESS, SCOTLAND
ISBN 978-1-84409-728-9

A CIP RECORD FOR THIS TITLE IS AVAILABLE FROM THE BRITISH LIBRARY.

PROOFREAD BY NICKY LEACH
DESIGN BY LUCY BYATT
PRINTED AND BOUND IN THE EU

PUBLISHED BY FINDHORN PRESS
DELFT COTTAGE, DYKE,
FORRES IV36 2TF,
SCOTLAND, UK
TEL +44(0)1309-690582
FAX +44(0)131-777-2711
FINDHORNPRESS.COM
INFO@FINDHORNPRESS.COM

DISCLAIMER

OPENING2INTUITION, LUCY BYATT &
KIM ROBERTS, OFFER THEIR WORK FOR
YOUR PLEASURE & ENTERTAINMENT. AS
ARTISTS & CREATORS, WE BELIEVE THAT
THROUGH OUR OWN EXPERIENCES OUR
IDEAS ARE WORTHY OF PUBLICATION
& PRESENTATION. WE ADVISE YOU NOT
TO USE THIS WORK AS AN ALTERNATIVE
TO PRACTICAL MEDICINE OR MENTAL
& EMOTIONAL HEALTH CARE. WE ALSO
SUGGEST YOU DO NOT DRIVE DURING
OR IMMEDIATELY AFTER DOING ANY
OF THESE EXERCISES. HOWEVER, WE
DO URGE YOU TO ENJOY, EXPAND AND
BECOME CONSCIOUS OF THE BEAUTIFUL
SPIRIT THAT YOU TRULY ARE.

CONTENTS

PART 1

PART 2

ALL TEMPLATES IN THIS BOOK,
AS WELL AS THOSE IN BOOK 4,
CAN BE DOWNLOADED IN ONE GO AT
ganxy.com/i/116634

INTRODUCTION

CHAPTER 1

INTRODUCTION TO PSYCHIC ART

PSYCHIC ART IS THE PROCESS WHERE SOMEONE WORKS INTUITIVELY, USING DRAWING AND COLOUR TO COMMUNICATE PSYCHIC MESSAGES.

HI, I'VE COME FOR A READING.

A PSYCHIC ARTIST WILL OFTEN USE COLOUR...

...TO SHOW WHAT THEY ARE PICKING UP INTUITIVELY IN THEIR PSYCHIC READING.

OPENING2INTUITION'S HEART TEMPLATE HAS BEEN SPECIFICALLY DESIGNED FOR GENERAL PSYCHIC READINGS ABOUT LIFE.

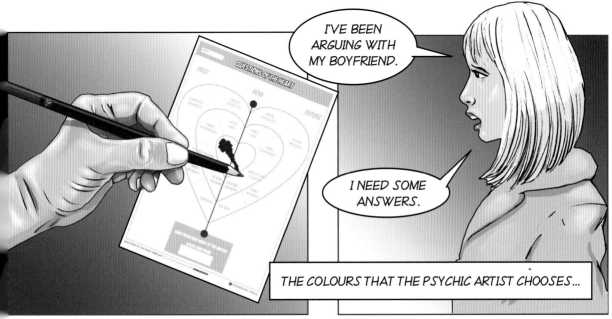

I'VE BEEN ARGUING WITH MY BOYFRIEND.

I NEED SOME ANSWERS.

THE COLOURS THAT THE PSYCHIC ARTIST CHOOSES...

CHAPTER 2

THE LANGUAGE OF COLOUR

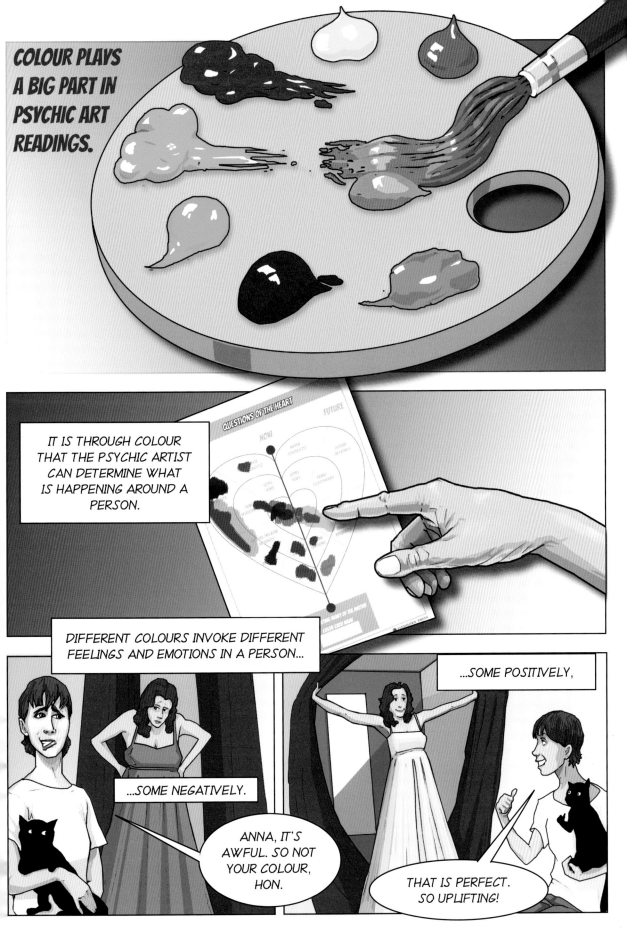

DIFFERENT COLOURS HAVE DIFFERENT MEANINGS WHEN IT COMES TO PSYCHIC ART READINGS.

GREEN CAN SYMBOLIZE GROWTH AND NEW OPPORTUNITIES.

COLOURS LIKE BRIGHT GREEN AND BRIGHT YELLOW NATURALLY GIVE A POSITIVE IMPRESSION AND FEELING.

WHILE A COLLECTION OF MURKY COLOURS...

...CAN TEND TO BRING MORE NEGATIVE FEELINGS.

HOW DOES COLOUR MAKE YOU FEEL?

DATE:

GO TO ganxy.com/i/116634 TO DOWNLOAD THIS TEMPLATE

THIS EXERCISE IS DESIGNED TO GET YOU THINKING ABOUT COLOUR AND HOW DIFFERENT COLOURS INVOKE DIFFERENT FEELINGS.

TAKE A MOMENT TO STUDY THE COLOURS SHOWN IN THE DIFFERENT BOXES BELOW ON THIS WORKSHEET.

LOOK AT EACH COLOUR AND SEE WHAT FEELINGS THAT COLOUR BRINGS UP FOR YOU.

MAKE A NOTE BENEATH EACH COLOUR DESCRIBING THE FEELINGS THAT COME UP FOR YOU.

MUSTARD

RED

GREEN

GRAY

PURPLE

PINK

TEMPLATE © LUCY BYATT & KIM ROBERTS 2011 OPENING2INTUITION FINDHORN PRESS

CHAPTER 3

USING COLOUR IN PSYCHIC ART READINGS

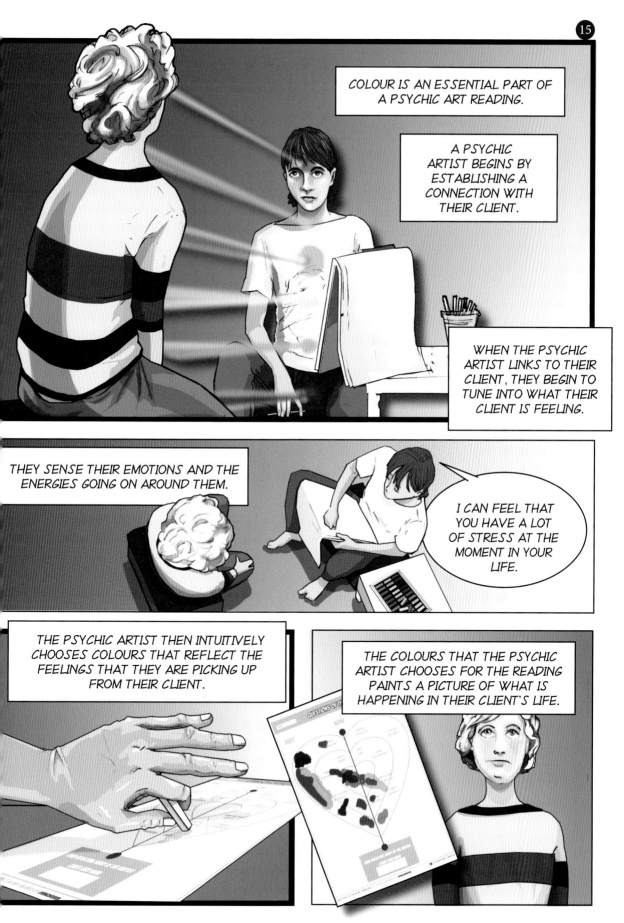

THE PSYCHIC ARTIST THEN LOOKS AT THE COLOURS THEY HAVE USED IN THEIR READING AND INTERPRETS THEM.

THIS RED SHOWS ME THAT YOU HAVE HAD SOME RECENT HEARTACHE.

YES, I'VE JUST BEEN DIVORCED.

A PSYCHIC ARTIST WILL OFTEN USE A NUMBER OF COLOURS, AND EACH OF THESE COLOURS WILL REVEAL DIFFERENT INFORMATION TO THE CLIENT.

YOU DO HAVE A RELATIONSHIP IN THE FUTURE. THE LIGHT ORANGE SHOWS ME THAT IT WILL BE A RELATIONSHIP WHERE YOU CAN DISCUSS YOUR FEELINGS EASILY.

AS WELL AS THE CHOICE OF COLOUR IN A READING, THE TEXTURE AND THE WAY THAT A PSYCHIC ARTIST DRAWS THEIR LINES AND COLOURS ALSO REVEAL DETAILS ABOUT THE CLIENT.

SMOOTH EVEN LINES CAN SUGGEST HARMONY AND BALANCE.

BROKEN LINES CAN SUGGEST DISHARMONY AND UNBALANCED ENERGY.

CHAPTER 4

COLOURFUL DIVINATION CARDS

THE RAINBOW ORACLE CARDS

THE RAINBOW ORACLE CARDS

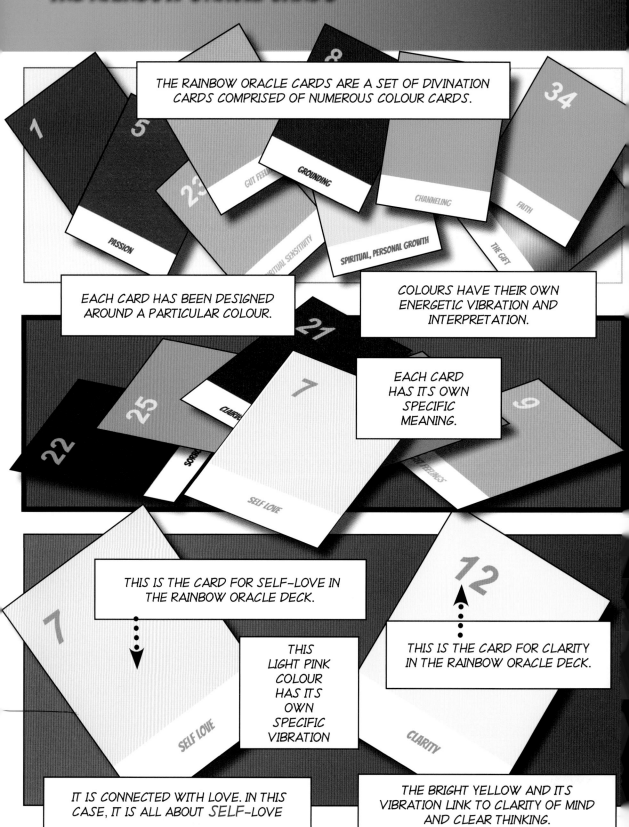

THE RAINBOW ORACLE CARDS ARE A SET OF DIVINATION CARDS COMPRISED OF NUMEROUS COLOUR CARDS.

EACH CARD HAS BEEN DESIGNED AROUND A PARTICULAR COLOUR.

COLOURS HAVE THEIR OWN ENERGETIC VIBRATION AND INTERPRETATION.

EACH CARD HAS ITS OWN SPECIFIC MEANING.

THIS IS THE CARD FOR SELF-LOVE IN THE RAINBOW ORACLE DECK.

THIS LIGHT PINK COLOUR HAS ITS OWN SPECIFIC VIBRATION

THIS IS THE CARD FOR CLARITY IN THE RAINBOW ORACLE DECK.

IT IS CONNECTED WITH LOVE. IN THIS CASE, IT IS ALL ABOUT SELF-LOVE

THE BRIGHT YELLOW AND ITS VIBRATION LINK TO CLARITY OF MIND AND CLEAR THINKING.

WORKING WITH THE RAINBOW ORACLE CARDS

THE CARDS HAVE BEEN DESIGNED TO BE USED (ON THEIR OWN) AND ALONGSIDE THE PSYCHIC ART READINGS THAT YOU WILL LEARN ABOUT IN THIS BOOK.

YOU CAN WORK WITH THE CARDS INDIVIDUALLY TO CONNECT TO EACH SPECIFIC COLOUR VIBRATION.

WORKING WITH COLOUR IN THIS WAY CAN BE VERY POWERFUL AND TRANSFORMATIVE.

I'M SORRY MARSHA – LAST IN, FIRST OUT!

HOW AM I GOING TO AFFORD CHRISTMAS?

WHEN LIFE IS VERY STRESSFUL WE CAN LOSE FAITH IN OURSELVES.

I THINK YOU WOULD REALLY BENEFIT FROM WORKING WITH THE COLOUR VIBRATIONS.

I WANT A BIG FAT TURKEY FOR CHRISTMAS!

USING THE RAINBOW ORACLE CARDS AND WORKING WITH COLOURS AND THEIR VIBRATIONS CAN BE VERY HEALING.

LET ME SHOW YOU HOW TO WORK WITH THE RAINBOW ORACLE CARDS.

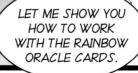

USING COLOUR VIBRATIONS TO HEAL

TAKE A MOMENT TO GO AND LOOK AT THE CARDS IN YOUR RAINBOW ORACLE DECK.

PICK A CARD THAT YOU FEEL RESONATES WITH YOU

YOU HAVE DRAWN THIS CARD BECAUSE YOU NEED THIS SOFT PINK COLOUR VIBRATION TO NURTURE YOURSELF.

FORM AN IMAGINARY BUBBLE AROUND YOURSELF.

TAKE YOUR CARD. TAKE A MOMENT TO LOOK AT IT AND CONNECT WITH THE COLOUR.

FILL THE BUBBLE WITH THE COLOUR ON YOUR CARD.

SELF-LOVE IS VERY IMPORTANT.

SURROUND YOURSELF WITH THIS COLOUR.

THIS PINK COLOUR HELPS YOU TO LOVE YOURSELF.

ALLOW THE COLOUR TO ENTER YOUR ENERGY FIELD.

SIT INSIDE YOUR BUBBLE FOR A FEW MINUTES, FOCUSING ON HOW THE COLOUR MAKES YOU FEEL.

HOW DOES IT INTERACT WITH YOUR ENERGY, AND HOW DOES IT MAKE YOU FEEL?

AFTER A FEW MINUTES, OPEN YOUR EYES. TURN YOUR ATTENTION TO YOUR FEET. IMAGINE SENDING IMAGINARY ROOTS DOWN THROUGH THE FLOOR INTO THE EARTH. DRAW THE EARTH ENERGY BACK INTO YOUR BODY AND GROUND YOURSELF.

WHAT COLOUR DID YOU PICK?

HOW DOES THE COLOUR MAKE YOU FEEL WHEN YOU LOOK AT IT?

HOW DID THE COLOUR FEEL WHEN YOU DID THE VISUALIZATION?

THREE-CARD READING

TRUST YOUR INTUITION. ALLOW IT TO GUIDE YOU TO THE CARD THAT SPEAKS TO YOU

TAKE A MOMENT TO THINK ABOUT THE QUESTION THAT YOU WANT TO ASK. WHEN YOU HAVE THE QUESTION, PICK UP YOUR CARDS AND HOLD THEM IN YOUR HANDS. FOCUS ON THE QUESTION AS YOU BEGIN TO CONNECT YOUR ENERGY WITH THE CARDS. BEGIN TO SHUFFLE YOUR CARDS AND SILENTLY ASK THE QUESTION IN YOUR MIND AS YOU DO THIS.

WHEN YOU FEEL READY, STOP SHUFFLING AND PLACE THE CARDS ON THE TABLE. FAN OUT THE CARDS WITH THE OPENING2INTUITION LOGO SIDE FACING UP.

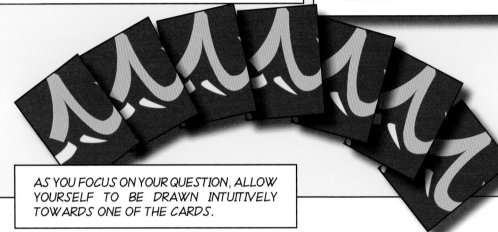

AS YOU FOCUS ON YOUR QUESTION, ALLOW YOURSELF TO BE DRAWN INTUITIVELY TOWARDS ONE OF THE CARDS.

TURN OVER THE FIRST CARD. PLACE THIS IN THE **PAST/QUESTIONS** BOX. THIS IS THE SITUATION AND THE ENERGY AROUND YOU IN THE PAST. IT WILL HELP YOU UNDERSTAND WHAT WAS SURROUNDING YOU THEN AND HOW THAT HAS AFFECTED YOU NOW. CONSULT THE GUIDEBOOK FOR THE MEANING OF THIS CARD.

TURN OVER THE SECOND CARD. PLACE THIS IN THE **PRESENT/CHALLENGE** BOX. YOU HAVE CHOSEN THIS CARD TO HIGHLIGHT THE CHALLENGES WITHIN YOUR QUESTION. THIS CAN BE IN A POSITIVE OR NEGATIVE WAY. CONSULT THE GUIDEBOOK FOR THE MEANING OF THIS CARD.

TURN OVER THE THIRD CARD. THIS CARD SHOWS THE POSSIBLE OUTCOME AT THIS TIME CONCERNING YOUR QUESTION. PLACE THIS CARD ON THE **FUTURE/OUTCOME** BOX. REMEMBER EVERY FUTURE IS CHANGED BY THE THOUGHTS AND DECISIONS THAT YOU MAKE IN YOUR PRESENT. CONSULT THE GUIDEBOOK FOR THE MEANING OF THE CARD.

CONSULT THE RAINBOW ORACLE CARD GUIDEBOOK FOR MORE INFORMATION ON THE CARDS THAT YOU HAVE DRAWN. IN THAT BOOKLET, YOU WILL BE GIVEN SOME GUIDANCE TO FOLLOW AND AN AFFIRMATION.

SAY YOUR AFFIRMATION TO YOURSELF THREE TIMES. THIS AFFIRMATION WILL HELP YOU TO FOCUS ON THE AREA OF YOUR LIFE THAT NEEDS HEALING. USE THE AFFIRMATION TO HELP CREATE A POSITIVE MINDSET AND TO EMPOWER YOU.

DATE:

QUESTION:

GO TO ganxy.com/i/116634 TO DOWNLOAD THIS TEMPLATE

PLACE CARD HERE
CARD NUMBER

COLOUR CARD NAME

PAST/QUESTION

PLACE CARD HERE
CARD NUMBER

COLOUR CARD NAME

PRESENT/CHALLENGE

PLACE CARD HERE
CARD NUMBER

COLOUR CARD NAME

FUTURE/OUTCOME

FINDHORN PRESS

ONE-CARD READING
TRUST YOUR INTUITION

TAKE A MOMENT TO THINK ABOUT THE QUESTION THAT YOU WANT TO ASK. WHEN YOU HAVE THE QUESTION, PICK UP YOUR CARDS AND HOLD THEM IN YOUR HANDS. FOCUS ON THE QUESTION AS YOU BEGIN TO CONNECT YOUR ENERGY WITH THE CARDS. BEGIN TO SHUFFLE YOUR CARDS AND SILENTLY ASK THE QUESTION IN YOUR MIND AS YOU DO THIS.

WHEN YOU FEEL READY, STOP SHUFFLING AND PLACE THE CARDS ON THE TABLE. FAN OUT THE CARDS WITH THE OPENING2INTUITION LOGO SIDE FACING UP.

AS YOU FOCUS ON YOUR QUESTION, ALLOW YOURSELF TO BE DRAWN INTUITIVELY TOWARDS ONE OF THE CARDS. ONE OF THE CARDS WILL STAND OUT MORE TO YOU. PICK UP THIS CARD.

TAKE THE CARD OUT, AND TURN IT OVER TO REVEAL THE COLOUR. READ THE WORD ON THE CARD, AND BEGIN TO FOCUS ON ANY THOUGHTS, FEELINGS, OR VISIONS THAT COME INTO YOUR MIND. ALLOW THIS INFORMATION TO FORM YOUR ANSWER.

CONSULT THE RAINBOW ORACLE CARD GUIDEBOOK FOR MORE INFORMATION ON THE CARD THAT YOU HAVE DRAWN. IN THAT BOOKLET, YOU WILL BE GIVEN SOME GUIDANCE TO FOLLOW AND AN AFFIRMATION.

SAY YOUR AFFIRMATION TO YOURSELF THREE TIMES. THIS AFFIRMATION WILL HELP YOU TO FOCUS ON THE AREA OF YOUR LIFE THAT NEEDS HEALING. USE THE AFFIRMATION TO HELP CREATE A POSITIVE MINDSET AND TO EMPOWER YOU.

ONE – CARD READING

DATE:

RELAX THEN FOCUS ON YOUR QUESTION:

GO TO ganxy.com/i/116634 TO DOWNLOAD THIS TEMPLATE

PLACE CARD HERE

CARD NUMBER

COLOUR CARD NAME

- COLOUR CARD NAME:

- SITUATION:

- FIRST IMPRESSIONS FROM CARD CHOICE:

WHAT WAS THE QUESTION?	HOW DOES THE COLOUR MAKE ME FEEL?	HOW DO I MOVE FORWARD?

PART 2

IN THIS SECTION OF THE BOOK,

YOU WILL LEARN ABOUT TWO DIFFERENT TYPES OF PSYCHIC ART READINGS...

...AND HOW TO DO THEM.

THE FIRST ONE IS A PSYCHIC ART PORTRAIT OF A SPIRIT GUIDE, WITH A READING.

THE SECOND IS A PSYCHIC ART READING USING A TEMPLATE TO DO A MORE GENERAL READING.

DRAWING YOUR SPIRIT GUIDE AND GIVING READINGS

upper world
steps
lower world
FIRST, YOU WILL GO ON A GUIDED VISUALIZATION TO THE UPPER WORLD, WHERE YOU WILL MEET YOUR SPIRIT GUIDE.
THEN YOU WILL LEARN HOW TO DRAW YOUR SPIRIT GUIDE.
my guide
my indian guide
YOU WILL WORK WITH SPECIALLY DESIGNED TEMPLATES TO DRAW YOUR SPIRIT GUIDE.
PSYCHIC PORTRAIT

CHAPTER 5

MEET YOUR SPIRIT GUIDE

IN THIS CHAPTER, YOU WILL LEARN HOW TO DO A GUIDED MEDITATION TO MEET YOUR SPIRIT GUIDE.

YOU WILL JOURNEY INTO THE TREE OF LIFE,

...AND BE GUIDED UP INTO THE UPPER WORLD WHERE YOU WILL MEET YOUR SPIRIT GUIDE.

FOR THIS SECTION OF THE BOOK,

WE RECOMMEND THAT YOU USE THE OPENING2INTUITION SHAMANIC HEALING CD.

OPENING *2intuition*

SHAMANIC HEALING

KAREN GRACE
voice & music

LUCY BYATT
illustrations

KIM ROBERTS
text

FIND A QUIET SPACE WHERE YOU WILL NOT BE INTERRUPTED. LIE DOWN ON THE FLOOR OR SIT DOWN IN A CHAIR AND SLOWLY BEGIN TO RELAX.

CLOSE YOUR EYES.

BEGIN TO INHALE DEEPLY AND EXHALE SOFTLY.

INHALE AND BREATHE IN HEALING WHITE LIGHT. FEEL IT ENTER YOUR BODY. THEN EXHALE AND RELEASE THROUGH THE OUT BREATH.

CALMNESS

WITH EACH OUT-BREATH, LET GO OF ANY TENSIONS AND STRAINS FROM THE DAY.

LISTEN TO THE SOUND OF THE VOICE ON THE CD AND/OR THE SOUND OF THE DRUM.

IMAGINE YOURSELF STANDING IN A BEAUTIFUL GREEN FIELD. IT IS A SUNNY DAY, THE SKY IS VIBRANT BLUE, AND EVERYTHING IS PEACEFUL.

YOU SEE A GIANT OAK TREE IN FRONT OF YOU. THE TREE IS LARGER THAN ANY TREE THAT YOU HAVE EVER SEEN BEFORE. IT HAS A THICK STRONG TRUNK AND LARGE ROOTS. ITS BRANCHES REACH HIGH INTO THE SKY.

AS YOU BEGIN TO WALK TOWARDS THE TREE YOU BECOME AWARE OF AN OPEN DOORWAY IN THE MIDDLE OF THE TREE.

STEP INTO THE ENTRANCE OF THE TREE.

INSIDE THE TREE, YOU SEE THAT EVERYTHING IS HOLLOW. THERE IS A WHOLE OTHER WORLD INSIDE THIS TREE.

A STAIRWAY LEADS UPWARDS AND ANOTHER STAIRWAY LEADS DOWNWARDS.

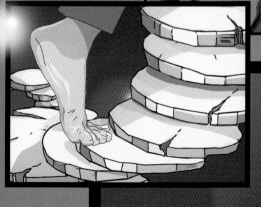

TAKE YOUR FIRST STEP ONTO THE STAIRCASE.

TAKE ANOTHER STEP UPWARDS NOW AND IMAGINE YOURSELF JOURNEYING HIGHER INTO THE TREE.

FEEL YOURSELF GETTING MORE AND MORE RELAXED AS YOU STEP UPWARDS ONTO THE THIRD STEP.

ON THE 9TH STEP YOU NOTICE AN EXIT IN FRONT OF YOU.

AT THE

YOU SEE THE GATES TO THE UPPER WORLD IN FRONT OF YOU

YOU BEGIN TO FEEL THE WARM GLOW OF THE SUN BEAMING DOWN ON YOU FROM THE UPPER WORLD.

YOU JOURNEY CLOSER TO IT.

AT THE ENTRANCE GATES OF THE
UPPER WORLD. AN ANGEL OPENS THE
GATE AND LETS YOU STEP INSIDE.

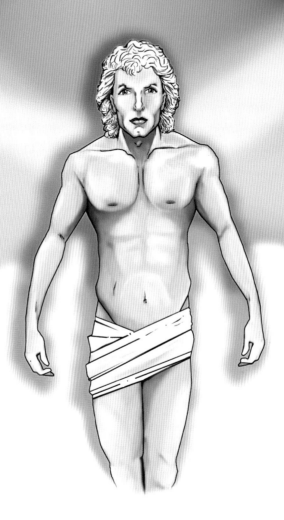

IT IS SO PEACEFUL HERE, AND
THE ENERGY IS SO HEALING

ALL AROUND YOU IS BEAUTIFUL.

YOU FEEL THE HEALING ENERGY,

IN FRONT OF YOU IS A MAGNIFICENT FAIRY TALE CASTLE WITH GOLDEN SPIRES THAT RISE HIGH INTO THE CLOUDS.

IMAGINE WALKING TO THE CASTLE NOW AND WALKING ALONG THE PATHWAY TO THE LARGE CASTLE DOOR.

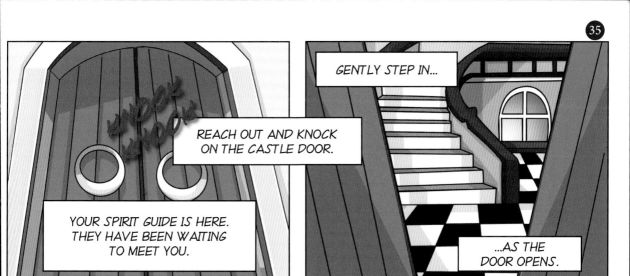

MEETING YOUR SPIRIT GUIDE

WAVE GOODBYE TO THE ANGELS AS YOU TAKE YOUR FIRST STEP BACK INTO THE TREE AND ONTO THE STAIRCASE.

SLOWLY BEGIN TO WALK DOWN THE STAIRS, COUNTING THE STEPS AS YOU GO. TEN. NINE. EIGHT. SEVEN. SIX. FIVE. FOUR. THREE. TWO. ONE.

YOU FIND YOURSELF AT THE BOTTOM OF THE TREE, AND WALK SLOWLY OUT OF THE TREE INTO THE MEADOW.

MEETING YOUR SPIRIT GUIDE

YOU ARE AT THE END OF YOUR JOURNEY NOW.

BEGIN TO BRING YOUR ATTENTION BACK TO YOUR BODY.

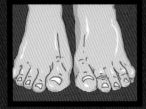

FEEL THE FLOOR BENEATH YOU.

WIGGLE YOUR TOES AND FINGERS SLOWLY BECOME MORE PRESENT.

BECOME AWARE OF THE ROOM.

TAKE YOUR TIME TO COME BACK.

SLOWLY OPEN YOUR EYES AND LOOK AROUND.

WE STRONGLY RECOMMEND THAT YOU LISTEN TO THE GROUNDING TRACK ON OUR STARTER CD TO HELP YOU GROUND YOURSELF.

CHAPTER 6

HOW TO DRAW YOUR SPIRIT GUIDE

SPIRIT GUIDE CHECKLIST

GO TO ganxy.com/i/116634 TO DOWNLOAD THIS TEMPLATE

WAS MY GUIDE MALE OR FEMALE?

WAS MY GUIDE HUMAN OR NON-HUMAN?

HOW OLD WAS MY GUIDE?

WHAT WAS MY GUIDE WEARING?

DID MY GUIDE HAVE ANY DISTINCTIVE FEATURES?

WHAT GIFT DID YOUR GUIDE GIVE YOU?

TEMPLATE © LUCY BYATT & KIM ROBERTS 2017 OPENING2INTUITION

FINDHORN PRESS

AFTER YOU HAVE COMPLETED YOUR VISUALIZATION TO MEET YOUR SPIRIT GUIDE, YOU CAN PREPARE TO DRAW YOUR GUIDE.

TAKE A MOMENT TO THINK ABOUT YOUR VISUALIZATION AND THE SPIRIT GUIDE THAT YOU JUST MET.

NOW GO THROUGH YOUR CHECKLIST.

WHEN YOU HAVE FINISHED YOUR JOURNEY VISUALISATION IT IS IMPORTANT TO FILL IN YOUR SPIRIT GUIDE CHECKLIST. YOU CAN THEN GATHER INFORMATION THAT IS EASILY FORGOTTEN.

USING RECORD SHEET 4 (PSYCHIC PORTRAIT) SHEET YOU CAN USE PENCILS TO DRAW THE INFORMATION THAT YOU HAVE GATHERED ABOUT YOUR GUIDE.

THE COLOURS YOU USE ARE REALLY IMPORTANT. THEY WILL GIVE YOU INFORMATION ABOUT YOUR SPIRIT GUIDE.

FOR EXAMPLE; IN FIG. 1, THE SAILOR IS WEARING A BROWN JUMPER. THE BROWN IS CLEAR AND NICELY SHADED, WHICH MEANS THAT THIS GUIDE WILL WORK WITH YOU TO MOVE FORWARD IN A PRACTICAL WAY. IT IS NOT ABOUT BEING BOGGED DOWN, IT IS ABOUT BE PRACTICALLY CREATIVE.

HIS HAT IS BLUE WITH A YELLOW BADGE. THIS INDICATES IDEAS BROUGHT THROUGH DURING DREAMS.

THIS GUIDE IS A SAILOR AND WILL HELP YOU NAVIGATE A PRACTICAL COURSE WITH YOUR READINGS. LISTEN TO YOUR DREAMS. YOU WILL FIND ANSWERS THERE.

fig 1.

WHEN YOU LOOK AT YOUR DRAWINGS, IT IS IMPORTANT TO READ ALL OF THE CLUES. SOME ARE OBVIOUS, AND SOME ARE HIDDEN. ONLY YOU WILL PICK THEM UP PSYCHICALLY.

IN FIG. 2, THE LADY HAS A PIECE OF GREEN JEWELLERY AT HER THROAT. THIS SHOWS THAT SHE SPEAKS FROM THE HEART. HER DRESS MAY BE BLACK, BUT THE BEAUTY OF BLACK IS THAT IT IS FILLED WITH POTENTIAL. HER LIPS ARE VERY RED. THIS WILL ASSIST YOU IN SPEAKING IN AN IMME-DIATE, STRAIGHTFORWARD WAY; AND BECAUSE SHE HAS THE GREEN JEW-EL AT HER THROAT, HER WORDS ARE TEMPERED.

HER HAIR IS BROWN, SO SHE IS GROUNDED AND THINKS THROUGH WHAT SHE SAYS.

fig 2.

IN FIG. 3; THE CHINESE GUIDE HAS A LOT OF RED. AS A GUIDE, HE BRINGS YOU ENERGY. IT WILL BE IMPORTANT TO TUNE IN TO THE STRENGTH AND ENERGY HE GIVES YOU BEFORE YOUR READINGS. HE IS ALSO WEARING A YELLOW HAT AND YELLOW AROUND HIS THROAT. HE IS KEEN FOR YOU TO USE WHEN YOU ARE TEACHING. HE WANTS TO PASS HIS WISDOM ON THROUGH YOU.

WHEN YOU ARE DRAWING GUIDES FOR OTHERS, BE AWARE THAT SOME OF THE TRAITS YOU DESCRIBE WITH YOUR COLOURS AND MARKS WILL DESCRIBE YOUR CLIENT, AS WELL AS THEIR GUIDES. THERE ARE ALWAYS CLUES IN DRAWINGS, AND NO MARK IS WASTED WHEN SPIRIT IS TRYING TO COMMUNICATE WITH YOU.

fig 3.

RECORD SHEET 04

PSYCHIC PORTRAIT

GO TO ganxy.com/i/116634 **TO DOWNLOAD THIS TEMPLATE**

PLACE CARD HERE

COLOR CARD NAME

FINDHORN PRESS

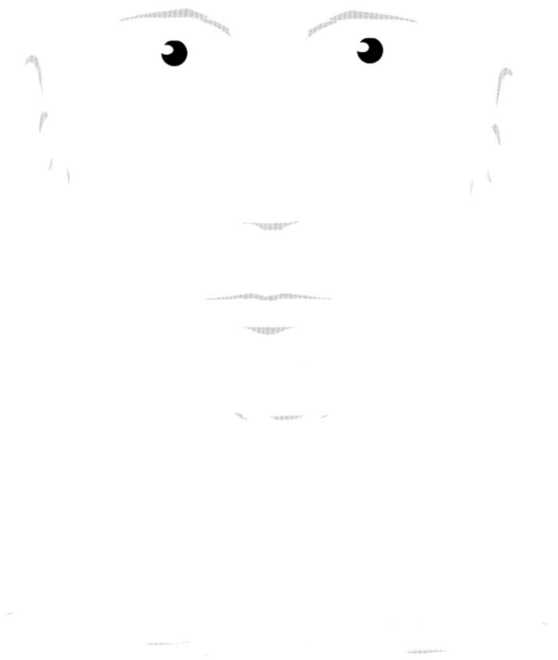

CHAPTER 7

USING THE HEART TEMPLATE

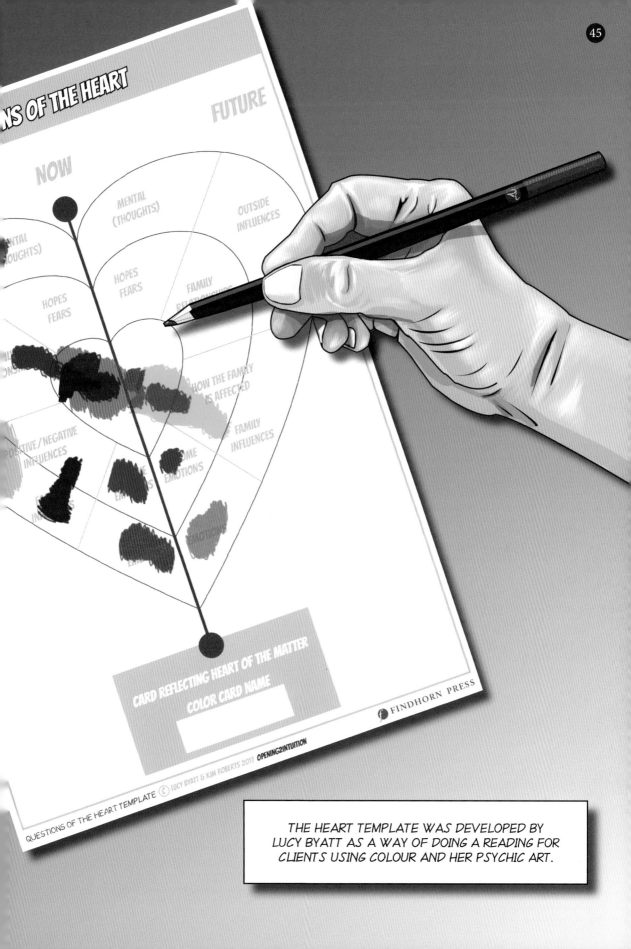

THE HEART TEMPLATE WAS DEVELOPED BY LUCY BYATT AS A WAY OF DOING A READING FOR CLIENTS USING COLOUR AND HER PSYCHIC ART.

...ESTIONS OF THE HEART

NOW

FUTURE

THE HEART TEMPLATE ALLOWS THE READER TO LOOK INTO THE HEART OF THE MATTER AROUND THEIR CLIENT.

IT IS A SIMPLE DIAGRAM OF A HEART DIVIDED INTO TWO HALVES.

OUTSIDE INFLUENCES

FAMILY RELATIONSHIPS

FAMILY RELATIONSHIPS

PAST

POSITIVE/NEGATIVE INFLUENCES

FROM THE FAMILY REFLECTED

FAMILY INFLUENCES

FAMILY INFLUENCES

NEGATIVE EMOTIONS

POSITIVE EMOTIONS

THE FIRST HALF OF THE HEART ON THE LEFT REPRESENTS THE PAST AND PAST EVENTS AND EMOTIONS AROUND THE PERSON HAVING THE READING.

THE MIDDLE LINE DRAWN THROUGH THE HEART REPRESENTS THE PRESENT DAY AND THE NOW.

CARD REFLECTING HEART OF THE MATTER

COLOR CARD NAME

FINDHORN PRESS

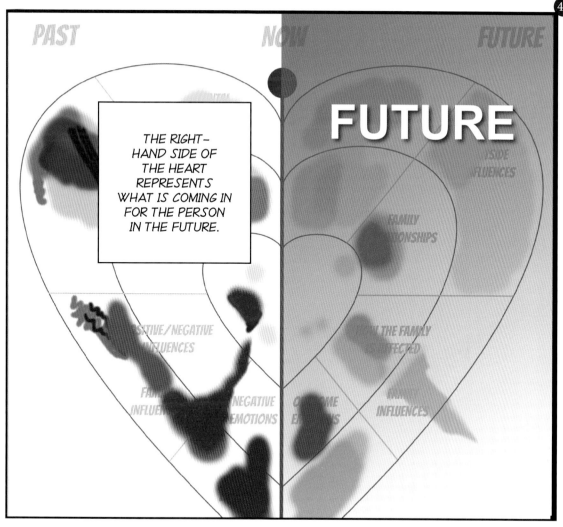

PAST   NOW   FUTURE

FUTURE

THE RIGHT-HAND SIDE OF THE HEART REPRESENTS WHAT IS COMING IN FOR THE PERSON IN THE FUTURE.

WHEN USING THE PSYCHIC HEART DIAGRAM, THE PSYCHIC ARTIST WILL USE COLOURS TO COLOUR THE TEMPLATE.

USING THE RAINBOW COLOUR CARDS WILL HELP YOU UNDERSTAND HOW TO COMMUNICATE WITH COLOUR MORE.

EACH COLOUR REPRESENTS DIFFERENT EMOTIONS AND FEELINGS.

QUESTIONS OF THE HEART

DATE:

PAST   **NOW**   **FUTURE**

OUTSIDE INFLUENCES

FAMILY RELATIONSHIPS

FAMILY RELATIONSHIPS

POSITIVE/NEGATIVE INFLUENCES

IS THE FAMILY AFFECTED

FAMILY INFLUENCES

NEGATIVE EMOTIONS

OUTCOME EMOTIONS

FAMILY INFLUENCES

THE PSYCHIC ARTIST INTUITIVELY CHOOSES THE COLOURS TO WHICH THEY ARE DRAWN.

THEY PLACE THE COLOURS IN THE AREA OF THE HEART TO WHICH THEY ARE DRAWN.

BY SENSING WHAT COLOURS WE HAVE USED, THE ANSWERS COME TO US. IN THE HEART CENTRE, FOR EXAMPLE, A RED SPLODGE WITH A DARKER LINE ON IT CAN INDICATE A DIVORCE, PAIN AND AN UNFAITHFULNESS. THE TWO LIGHTER PINKS IN THE HEART CAN INDICATE TWO GROWN CHILDREN. IN THE FUTURE THERE IS ANOTHER RELATIONSHIP ON THE HORIZON. IT IS AT THE FURTHER EDGES OF THE HEART SO IT IS A RELATIONSHIP THAT WILL COME WHEN THE TIME IS RIGHT AND AS IT IS TOUCHING ON THE FAMILY RELATIONSHIP BOX IT WILL AFFECT AND BE AFFECTED BT THE QUERENTS FAMILY. HOWEVER THERE ARE TWO SMALLER PINK DOTS INDICATING TWO SHORTER RELATIONSHIPS, ONE AFTER THE OTHER BEFORE THE CLIENT MEETS THIS MORE IMPORTANT RELATIONSHIP.

THE VARIOUS COLOURS THAT THE PSYCHIC ARTIST USES BUILD UP A COMPLETE COLOURED TEMPLATE AT THE END OF THE READING.

ONCE YOU HAVE YOUR COLOUR, TAKE A MOMENT TO TUNE IN TO IT INTUITIVELY.

COLOUR WILL TAKE ON A NEW MEANING WHEN IT IS PLACED AGAINST ANOTHER COLOUR.

YOURE JOB DURING A READING IS TO CREATE A COLOUR VOCABULARY THAT YOU CAN UNDERSTAND.

ONLY YOU CAN DECIDE HOW TO INTERPERATE THAT COLOUR, AND YOU HAVE TO TRUST YOURSELF.

BEFORE ANY READING, IT IS VERY IMPORTANT TO ASK YOUR GUIDES AND HELPERS TO HELP.

ASKING THEM TO HELP CONNECTS YOU WITH THE GUIDES AND HELPERS OF YOUR CLIENT.

THIS ENSURES THAT YOU ARE OPEN TO WHAT THE CLIENT NEEDS AND WANTS FROM THE READING.

ASKING WHAT THEY WANT AND NEED FROM SPIRIT IS REALLY IMPORTANT.

HOW TO DO A PSYCHIC ART READING USING THE HEART TEMPLATE

5 FOCUS ON CONNECTING TO YOUR CLIENT'S ENERGY.

SOLAR PLEXUS

SEND AN ENERGETIC THREAD FROM YOUR SOLAR PLEXUS INTO YOUR CLIENT'S AURA.

6 AS YOU LINK IN TO YOUR CLIENT, YOU WILL BEGIN TO SENSE THEIR ENERGY. WHEN THIS HAPPENS, YOU ARE READY TO BEGIN.

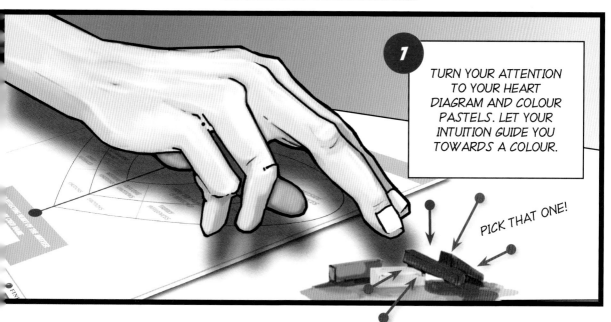

7 TURN YOUR ATTENTION TO YOUR HEART DIAGRAM AND COLOUR PASTELS. LET YOUR INTUITION GUIDE YOU TOWARDS A COLOUR.

PICK THAT ONE!

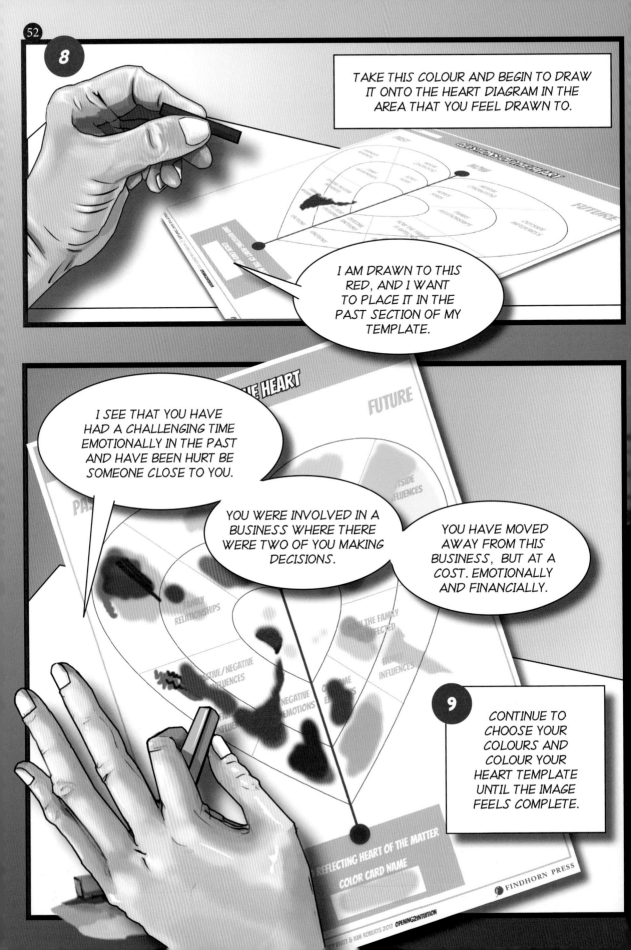

10

NOW TAKE A MOMENT TO LOOK AT THE COLOURED HEART DIAGRAM.

SENSE WHAT THEY MEAN TO YOUR CLIENT AND THEIR LIFE.

LOOK AT THE COLOURS, AND BEGIN TO TUNE IN TO THEM.

EACH COLOUR WILL BRING ITS OWN FEELING, AND AS YOU TUNE IN TO THE COLOUR, YOU MAY ALSO GET OTHER INFORMATION.

I SEE YOU MOVING HOUSE, MOVING TO A NEW BUILDING.

YOU MAY SEE IMAGES CLAIRVOYANTLY.

YOU MAY BE GIVEN WORDS CLAIRAUDIENTLY.

I'M HEARING THAT IT'S TIME FOR YOU TO BRANCH OUT ON YOUR OWN.

NOW IS A TIME TO FOCUS ON YOU,

WITHOUT A PARTNER!

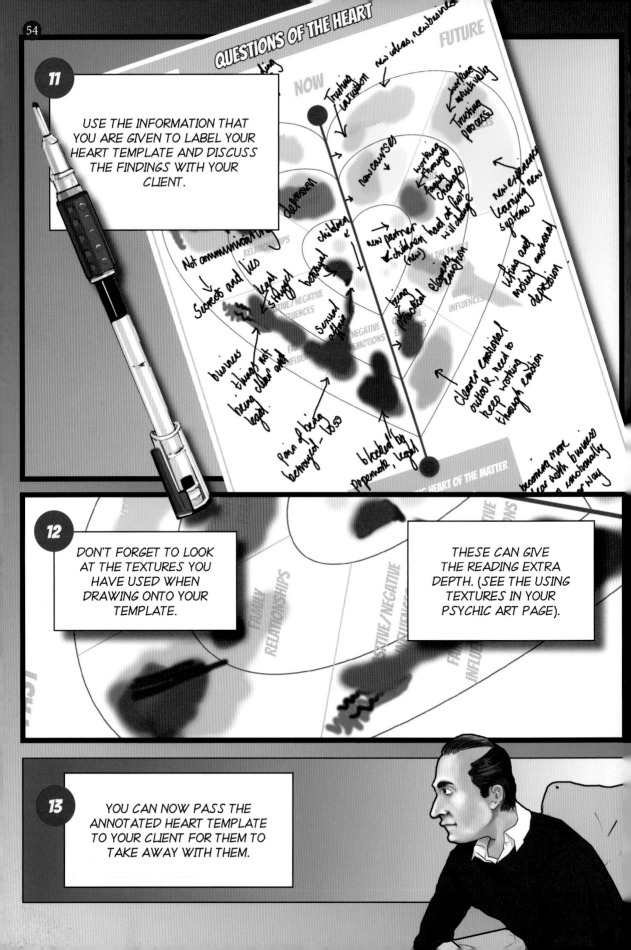

11 USE THE INFORMATION THAT YOU ARE GIVEN TO LABEL YOUR HEART TEMPLATE AND DISCUSS THE FINDINGS WITH YOUR CLIENT.

12 DON'T FORGET TO LOOK AT THE TEXTURES YOU HAVE USED WHEN DRAWING ONTO YOUR TEMPLATE.

THESE CAN GIVE THE READING EXTRA DEPTH. (SEE THE USING TEXTURES IN YOUR PSYCHIC ART PAGE).

13 YOU CAN NOW PASS THE ANNOTATED HEART TEMPLATE TO YOUR CLIENT FOR THEM TO TAKE AWAY WITH THEM.

14

SMUDGE YOUR ROOM TO CLEAR THE ENERGY AND PREPARE THE SPACE FOR YOUR NEXT READING

AFTER MOVING THROUGH THE ROOM WITH YOUR SMUDGE STICK, OPEN ANY WINDOWS AND ALLOW THE SMOKE TO CLEAR.

15

GROUND YOURSELF AND RECONNECT TO THE EARTH, SO YOU ARE READY TO MOVE ON TO THE NEXT TASK

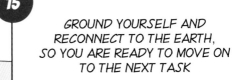

USE OUR GROUNDING EXERCISE FROM STARTER AUDIO-CD AND / OR OUR SMUDGING INFORMATION FROM OUR O2I SERIES BOOK 1.

CHAPTER 8

SAMPLE READINGS

QUESTIONS OF THE HEART

DATE:

GO TO ganxy.com/i/116634 TO DOWNLOAD THIS TEMPLATE

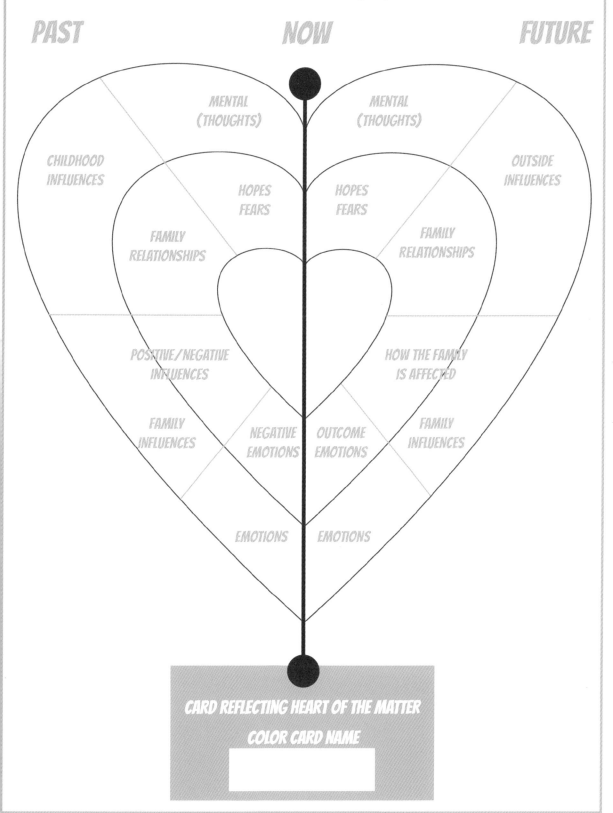

PAST   NOW   FUTURE

MENTAL (THOUGHTS)

MENTAL (THOUGHTS)

CHILDHOOD INFLUENCES

OUTSIDE INFLUENCES

HOPES FEARS

HOPES FEARS

FAMILY RELATIONSHIPS

FAMILY RELATIONSHIPS

POSITIVE/NEGATIVE INFLUENCES

HOW THE FAMILY IS AFFECTED

FAMILY INFLUENCES

NEGATIVE EMOTIONS

OUTCOME EMOTIONS

FAMILY INFLUENCES

EMOTIONS

EMOTIONS

CARD REFLECTING HEART OF THE MATTER

COLOR CARD NAME

TRANSLATING THE HEART TEMPLATE

LOOKING INTO THE PAST

THE LEFT HAND OF THE TEMPLATE IS BROKEN INTO A NUMBER OF SECTIONS. EVERYTHING THAT IS SHOWN ON THIS SIDE IS ROOTED IN THE PAST.

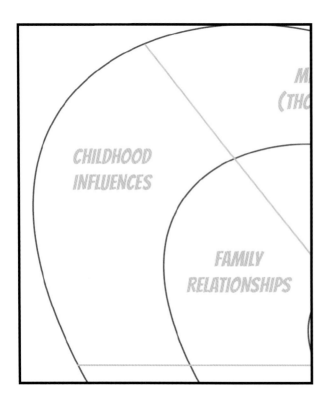

CHILDHOOD INFLUENCES

THIS SECTION OF THE HEART TEMPLATE DEALS WITH THE PERSON'S CHILDHOOD INFLUENCES. THIS INCLUDES WHERE THEY GREW UP, HOW THEY WERE SCHOOLED, WHO LOOKED AFTER THEM, AND HOW THEY WERE TREATED.

SOMEONE WHO HAS HAD A HAPPY CHILDHOOD WILL HAVE VERY POSITIVE COLOURS IN THIS SECTION OF THEIR CHART. SOMEONE WHO HAS HAD AN UNPLEASANT CHILDHOOD WILL HAVE MORE NEGATIVE COLOURS TO REFLECT THESE EXPERIENCES. SO YOU CAN USE THIS SECTION OF THE HEART TEMPLATE TO INTUITIVELY GAIN INSIGHT INTO A PERSON'S CHILDHOOD.

FAMILY RELATIONSHIPS

THIS SECTION OF THE HEART TEMPLATE REVEALS TO THE PSYCHIC ARTIST THE CLIENT'S FAMILY DYNAMIC AND EMOTIONAL HOME LIFE.

DIFFERENT COLOURS IN THIS SECTION OF THE CHART WILL REVEAL INFORMATION ABOUT THE FAMILY AND HOW IT HAS AFFECTED THE CLIENT IN THE PAST, AND IN SOME CASES, CONTINUES TO AFFECT THEM IN THE PRESENT.

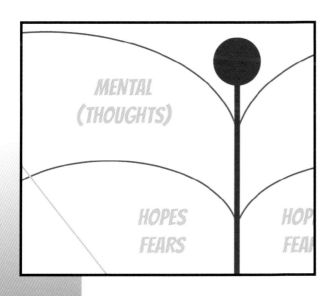

MENTAL THOUGHTS/ HOPES AND FEARS

THIS SECTION DEALS WITH PAST THOUGHT PATTERNS AN PROCESSES THAT THE CLIENT HAS HAD ABOUT LIFE. IT ALSO DEALS WITH THEIR PAST HOPES AND FEARS.

SOMETIMES YOU CAN FIND THAT NEGATIVE THOUGHT PATTERNS FROM THE PAST CAN BLOCK THE CLIENT FROM MOVING FORWARD. BY SHOWING THEM THESE BLOCKS IN A READING WE CAN BRING HEALING TO THE SITUATION AND CHANGE THE THOUGHT PATTERNS.

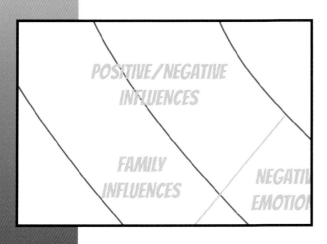

FAMILY & POSITIVE /NEGATIVE INFLUENCES

THIS SECTION LOOKS AT VARIOUS INFLUENCES AROUND THE CLIENT'S CHILDHOOD.

THESE INCLUDE:
- SCHOOL
- FRIENDS AND PEER GROUP
- HOW OTHER PEOPLE VIEW THEM
- POPULARITY
- HOBBIES AND INTERESTS
- SIBLING RELATIONSHIPS

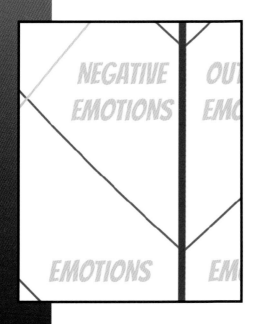

EMOTIONS

THIS SECTION DEALS WITH WHAT THE CLIENT IS HOLDING ONTO EMOTIONALLY FROM THE PAST.

THESE EMOTIONS CAN BE POSITIVE OR NEGATIVE AND ARE USUALLY CARRIED THROUGH TO ADULTHOOD.

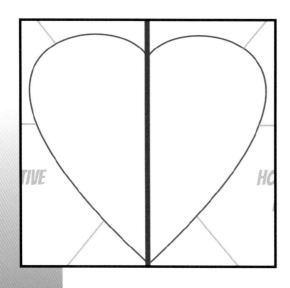

THE CENTRE OF THE HEART

THE CENTRE OF THE HEART REPRESENTS THE PERSON'S INTIMATE RELATIONSHIPS. IT ALSO SHOWS PARENTAL CONNECTIONS AND INFORMATION ABOUT A CLIENT'S CHILDREN. IT IS DIVIDED INTO TWO HALVES – THE PAST AND THE FUTURE – WITH THE LINE BEING THE PRESENT.

LOOKING INTO THE FUTURE

THE RIGHT HAND OF THE TEMPLATE IS BROKEN INTO A NUMBER OF SECTIONS. EVERYTHING THAT IS SHOWN ON THIS SIDE SHOWS A POSSIBLE FUTURE.

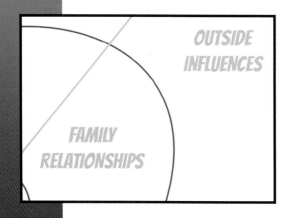

FAMILY RELATIONSHIP/ OUTSIDE INFLUENCES

THIS PART OF THE HEART TEMPLATE LOOKS AT YOUR FAMILY RELATIONSHIPS, YOUR CHILDREN, AND THE CHILDREN OF OTHERS AROUND YOU. IT IS ALSO ABOUT WHO YOU SOCIALIZE WITH AND WHO YOU CREATE A FAMILY WITH.

THE OUTSIDE INFLUENCES ARE THE PEOPLE YOU WORK AND DO BUSINESS WITH.

MENTAL THOUGHTS/ HOPES AND FEARS

THIS SECTION DEALS WITH FUTURE THOUGHT PATTERNS AND PROCESSES THAT THE CLIENT WILL HAVE ABOUT THEIR LIFE. IT ALSO DEALS WITH FUTURE HOPES AND FEARS.

IT CAN SHOW A POSSIBLE FUTURE FOR THE CLIENT, DEPENDING ON THEIR THOUGHT PROCESSES.

HOW THE FAMILY IS AFFECTED / FAMILY INFLUENCES

THIS PART OF THE HEART TEMPLATE LOOKS AT YOUR FAMILY RELATIONSHIPS, YOUR CHILDREN, AND THE CHILDREN OF OTHERS AROUND YOU. IT IS ALSO ABOUT WHO YOU SOCIALIZE WITH AND WHO YOU CREATE A FAMILY WITH.

THIS IS HOW THEY ARE AFFECTED BY YOUR PRESENT AND FUTURE DECISIONS.

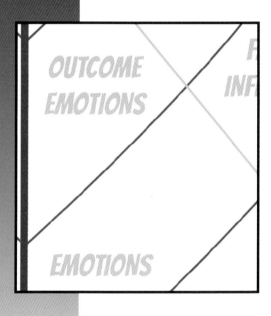

EMOTIONS

THIS SECTION DEALS WITH THINGS THE CLIENT COULD BE EXPERIENCING EMOTIONALLY IN THE FUTURE.

THESE EMOTIONS CAN BE POSITIVE OR NEGATIVE AND ARE USUALLY HOW WE FEEL ABOUT THE QUESTION.

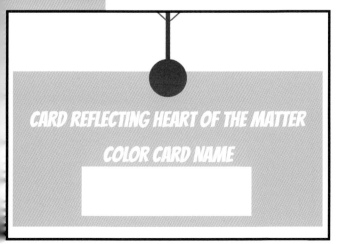

RAINBOW ORACLE COLOUR CARD

USING THE RAINBOW ORACLE, YOU CAN INTUITIVELY PICK A CARD FROM THE PACK. THIS CHOSEN COLOUR CARD REFLECTS THE WHOLE READING. YOU CAN USE THE RAINBOW ORACLE GUIDEBOOK TO GAIN FURTHER UNDERSTANDING.

EXERCISE PRACTICE READING

IN THIS SECTION, YOU CAN PRACTICE INTERPRETING A COMPLETED HEART TEMPLATE. HERE, YOU ARE GOING TO BE LOOKING AT DIFFERENT COLOURS AND INTUITIVELY FEELING INTO WHAT THEY MEAN TO YOU.

AS YOU LOOK AT EACH COLOUR, ALLOW YOURSELF TO WITNESS ANY SENSATIONS THAT PARTICULAR COLOURS BRING UP FOR YOU. THIS WILL HELP YOU WITH TRANSLATING THE ENERGIES AROUND THE PERSON THAT ARE REFLECTED IN THE COLOURS THE PSYCHIC ARTIST USED TO DO THE READING.

SOME COLOURS YOU WILL ALWAYS ASSOCIATE WITH A MEANING; OTHER COLOURS MAY HAVE OTHER MEANINGS AND BE MORE FLUID.

WHEN YOU PUT THEM TOGETHER, YOU FORM A SPECIFIC COLOUR SCHEME THAT SHOWS THE ENERGY AROUND A PERSON.

WHILE USING THIS SAMPLE READING, IT'S IMPORTANT TO REMEMBER THAT DURING A READING YOU WILL BE BASING YOUR ANSWERS ON A REAL PERSON AND THEIR ENERGY AT THE TIME.

63

FILL IN YOUR INTERPRETATION OF THE COLOURS

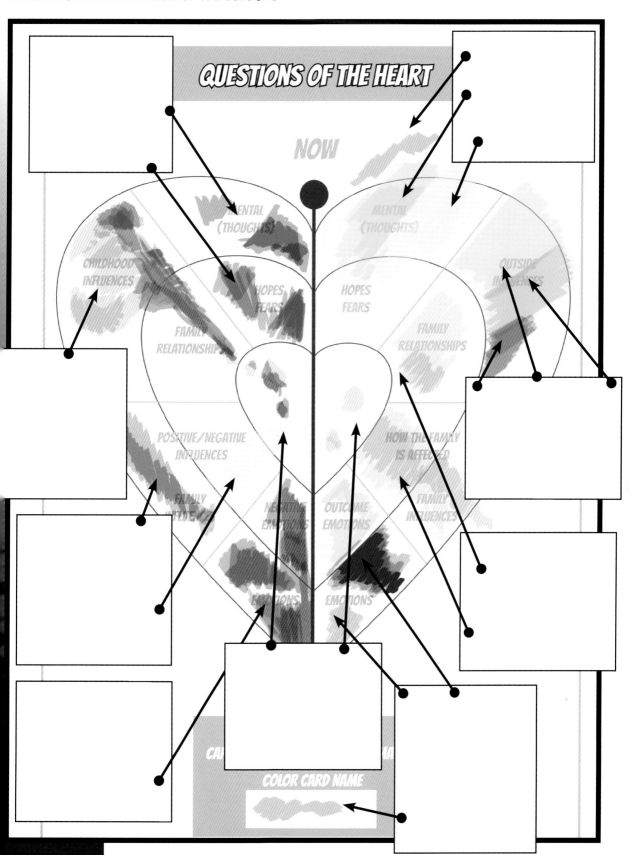

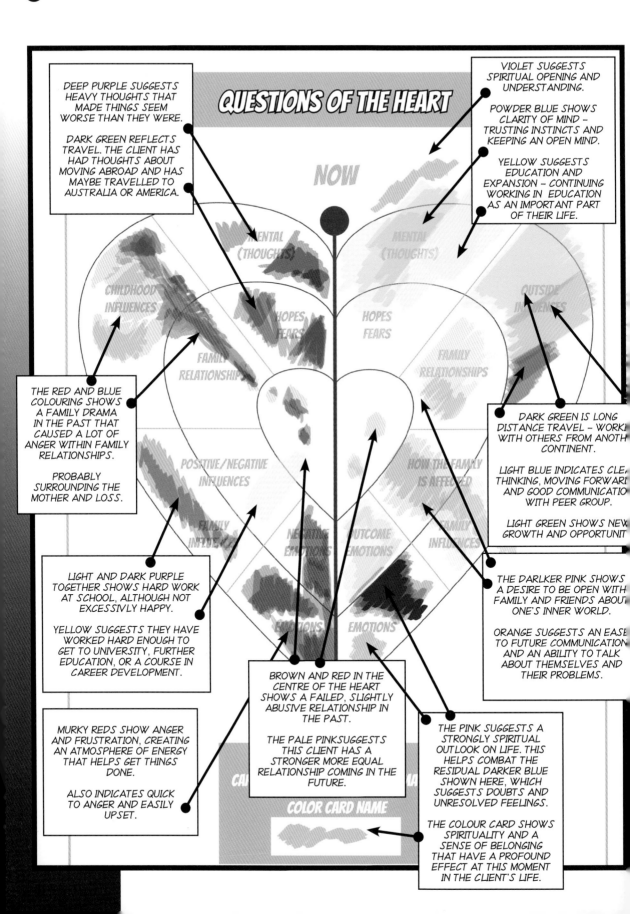

QUESTIONS OF THE HEART

DEEP PURPLE SUGGESTS HEAVY THOUGHTS THAT MADE THINGS SEEM WORSE THAN THEY WERE.

DARK GREEN REFLECTS TRAVEL. THE CLIENT HAS HAD THOUGHTS ABOUT MOVING ABROAD AND HAS MAYBE TRAVELLED TO AUSTRALIA OR AMERICA.

VIOLET SUGGESTS SPIRITUAL OPENING AND UNDERSTANDING.

POWDER BLUE SHOWS CLARITY OF MIND – TRUSTING INSTINCTS AND KEEPING AN OPEN MIND.

YELLOW SUGGESTS EDUCATION AND EXPANSION – CONTINUING WORKING IN EDUCATION AS AN IMPORTANT PART OF THEIR LIFE.

THE RED AND BLUE COLOURING SHOWS A FAMILY DRAMA IN THE PAST THAT CAUSED A LOT OF ANGER WITHIN FAMILY RELATIONSHIPS.

PROBABLY SURROUNDING THE MOTHER AND LOSS.

DARK GREEN IS LONG DISTANCE TRAVEL – WORKI WITH OTHERS FROM ANOTH CONTINENT.

LIGHT BLUE INDICATES CLE. THINKING, MOVING FORWARI AND GOOD COMMUNICATIO WITH PEER GROUP.

LIGHT GREEN SHOWS NEW GROWTH AND OPPORTUNIT

LIGHT AND DARK PURPLE TOGETHER SHOWS HARD WORK AT SCHOOL, ALTHOUGH NOT EXCESSIVLY HAPPY.

YELLOW SUGGESTS THEY HAVE WORKED HARD ENOUGH TO GET TO UNIVERSITY, FURTHER EDUCATION, OR A COURSE IN CAREER DEVELOPMENT.

THE DARLKER PINK SHOWS A DESIRE TO BE OPEN WITH FAMILY AND FRIENDS ABOU ONE'S INNER WORLD.

ORANGE SUGGESTS AN EASE TO FUTURE COMMUNICATION AND AN ABILITY TO TALK ABOUT THEMSELVES AND THEIR PROBLEMS.

MURKY REDS SHOW ANGER AND FRUSTRATION, CREATING AN ATMOSPHERE OF ENERGY THAT HELPS GET THINGS DONE.

ALSO INDICATES QUICK TO ANGER AND EASILY UPSET.

BROWN AND RED IN THE CENTRE OF THE HEART SHOWS A FAILED, SLIGHTLY ABUSIVE RELATIONSHIP IN THE PAST.

THE PALE PINKSUGGESTS THIS CLIENT HAS A STRONGER MORE EQUAL RELATIONSHIP COMING IN THE FUTURE.

THE PINK SUGGESTS A STRONGLY SPIRITUAL OUTLOOK ON LIFE. THIS HELPS COMBAT THE RESIDUAL DARKER BLUE SHOWN HERE, WHICH SUGGESTS DOUBTS AND UNRESOLVED FEELINGS.

THE COLOUR CARD SHOWS SPIRITUALITY AND A SENSE OF BELONGING THAT HAVE A PROFOUND EFFECT AT THIS MOMENT IN THE CLIENT'S LIFE.